Songs from My Minds Tree

2

Songs from My Minds Tree

Poems by

Jonel Abellanosa

Clare Songbirds
Publishing House

Clare Songbirds Publishing House Poetry Series

ISBN 978-1-947653-19-1
Songs From My Mind's Tree © 2018 Jonel Abellanosa

All Rights Reserved. Clare Songbirds Publishing House retains right to reprint.

Permission to reprint individual poems must be obtained from the author who owns the copyright.

Printed in the United States of America
FIRST EDITION

Clare Songbirds Publishing House
140 Cottage Street
Auburn, New York 13021
www.ClareSongbirdspub.com

Contents

Ode to the Sun	1
Man Born Blind	2
According to the Leaves	3
Empath	4
To Light	5
The River Speaks	6
Ode to the Holy Spirit	7
To the Miracle Plant	8
On the Balcony	9
To the Red Fire Monkey	10
Archivist	11
Teacher	12
Poetics	13
Homer	14
Healer	15
Riddle	16
Kite	17
The Soloist	18
One	19
Ode to Green Tea	20
Echo	21
Thirteen Ways of Looking	22
Flute for His Newborn	24
Tao of Indoor Walk	25
Nonfiction	26
Lovers in a Fresco	27
In My View	28
Piano	29
Storm	30
The Great Barrier Reef	31
Pictures of the Floating World	32
Ode to the Moon	37

The author wishes to thank the following publications where the poems first appeared:

The McNeese Review (McNeese State University, Louisiana) – "Ode to the Moon"
Windhover Journal of Christian Literature (University of Mary Hardin Baylor) – "Man Born Blind"
Penwood Review – "According to the Leaves,"
Poetry Kanto (Kanto Gakuin University, Japan) – "Empath" "Healer"
Birdsong Poets Anthology – "To Light"
Setu Magazine – "The River Speaks," "To the Miracle Plant"
Spirit Fire Review – "Ode to the Holy Spirit" (nominated for the Pushcart Prize)
The Penmen Review (Southern New Hampshire University) – "On the Balcony," "In My View"
The Camel Saloon – "One"
Rattle: "To the Red Fire Monkey"
The Peacock Journal – "Teacher"
Episteme Literary Journal (Bharat College, India): "Poetics"
Redbird Chapbooks – "Homer"
Filipino American Artist Directory – "Riddle"
Otoliths – "Kite"
Liquid Imagination – "The Soloist"
Anak Sastra: Stories from Southeast Asia – "Ode to Green Tea," "Flute for His Newborn"
Indiana Voice Journal – "Echo"
Marsh Hawk Review – "Thirteen Ways of Looking"
Allegro Poetry Journal – "Tao of Indoor Walk"
Inkscrawl – "Nonfiction"
The Literary Hatchet – "Lovers in a Fresco"
Poetry Quarterly – "Piano"
Spillwords – "Storm"
Cha: An Asian Literary Journal – "Pictures of the Floating World"
Dark Matter Literary Journal – "Ode to the Moon"
Blue Heron Review – "The Great Barrier Reef"

For Dexter, My Beloved Dalmatian
(2009 - December 25, 2017)

Ode to the Sun

Aphelion, as when I'm away brooding or
Basking, questions like corona. My bones
Crave strength, your morning flares like
Dandelions, neighborhood waking with joggers,
Early sizzling of pans in corner stores. I follow the
Familiar with rubber shoes, circling like my mind's
Gnomon. Running stirs imagination – a
Heliotrope. After an hour of exercises and recalls
I retreat to my room, in shadows, brew
Jasmine tea, in my poetry's woods reshaping
Knots, feel rejuvenation in my veins, your
Light like blood to organs. I invoke your
Melodies, secrets of magnifying life,
Noting how movements turn familiar
Or varied. I often doubt my descriptions like
Partial eclipses, as if unknowns bring me to
Quiet. These moments glow as silks of
Reticence, introversion like books in boxes,
Spaces longing to be ordered. I picture
Transformations in your touches, echo the
Unpurified but also labor for the true in my
Visualizations, trusting your revelations.
Wise bestower, grant me seeing and
Extend my understanding. I dwell in
Your colors, angling this glass to your
Zenith – to filter your tenderest sparkles

MAN BORN BLIND
John 9:1-12

We are all born of light.
Before I washed the mud
Formed with his saliva off my eyes
In the pool of Siloam, there were glimmers
Like rose petals on shiny black stone,
Temple-bound sandals stirring desert yellow,
Mists of green if I sensed a pit nearby.
When I smelled the coming rain
Blue hands claimed the dark.

Lights shape fuller than touch, sunder
Slants of seeing to rapture: illumination
Bending with the jar's belly, shimmering
Warmth from the cup's eddies, sheen
Of bones on papyrus, magnifying revelations.
As if it weren't enough, smells grew wings,
Singing like cherubs, one note above colors.
They who knew I wasn't born with
The gift of sight shared their amazement –
Cakes of pressed figs and raisin, lamb meat
Roasted with bitter herbs, unleavened bread.
Wine perfumed the courtyard. I entered
A room with a lady for the first time.

I couldn't miss it anymore: home-nurtured
Radiance, love's reflections, care thicker
Than water, glaring everywhere I looked,
Sending me back to starless corners.
After the crucifixion they said he lives
In a believer's heart, but this is how
Need folds night's veil of distance:
Eye contact, lamp of touch.

According to the Leaves

These, in clay-brown pots,
To the grotto, growing leaves
Like palms raised in prayer

These, lanceolate-thin,
Tapering acerose
Clustered like candles

Moringa saplings
Orbicular foliage
Reflecting like paten

Bougainvillea bonsais
Ovate, elliptic foliation
Like chalices

Greens in stems
Of light, the morning
All-embracing

In these arrangements:
Just another intuitive,
Contemplative, moment

I take a seat on the patio
In the middle of silence,
Shades

Is this delight, the spirit's
Earnest to be where
Wind might be seen?

Nothing shapes
The wind's melodies
Like swaying leaves

Suddenly I know:
This ornamentation, this time

Empath

Amplified, everything my senses apprehend:
Bitter-sweet, raindrops, chirps, scented air.
Colors and shapes crave my crowded vision,
Draining me to exhaustion. Same as the human:
Exposed to the heart's elements, I'm wind-borne,
Forged in strange behaviors. I see recognition as
Grooving tool, moments not mine to enjoy,
Hypnotized easily by my own thoughts
Into fallen leaves. Anxieties orphan me if I
Join otherness, my mind in a distant bench.
Keenness kindles with masquerades of
Loneliness. I realize I'm not alone. I
May know the next few days, but seldom come
Nearer to introduce myself and sound silly.
Overcoming the need to cry has stoned the
Pains I wear like gloves and raincoat, people
Quieter than inner conflicts. I struggle to
Realign gazes with what I see in couples
Strolling in the absence of time, forgetting
Trees and how they smiled earlier.
Under enormities of unease, I feel
Vulnerable like veils clouds keep lifting.
Wheeled in phobias, bending hours
Exfoliate my equanimity, and I grow cold,
Yearning for my room, begging my ears'
Zinging to stop, for silence and the void

To Light

A miracle of iridescence, the way the early sun
Brocades, trees greeting with winged singsongs,
Celebrating your return. I still as silence to the
Dawn's narration, watching transformations, the
Evincing, the world wearing colors, breathing
Fluorescing with your arrival. I've been studying
Glasses, your bents of reflections, means you
Hinge curvatures, transparencies of dwelling
Inward. This starapple in my hand, like a violet
Jewel I angle to your touches, turning it like a
Kaleidoscope. Your companionship with time
Limns my awareness. Luminosity lifts a winged
Marvel, making me see that butterfly enter the
Numinous, white and yellow wings pleasantly
Ordinary, or it is your will that complexity be
Perfected in the quotidian; yet flutters become
Quaint, leaf to leaf or petal to petal flitting
Reminding me of pages turning. It appears
Seeing is a glowing of flaws, the tiger orchid
True to its blemishes and the butterfly effect on
Understanding. It reminds of a flawed poem,
Visualizations ordered in imperfections. The
Wonder of insight refuses the perfect, the same
Extolment seen only when you shift with the
Yearn that flits again, as though the numinous
Zenith isn't a place but the constant unfolding

The River Speaks

Poet, it's easy to mistake my meanderings
As the convex-concave transit of past
And future. Why you're not God looking
From above. Paddling through my music
Makes you a participant. Somewhere
Along smoothened rustles the sun scatters
Small glass shards, little golden vanishings.
If you persevere, you'll see the ancient tree
On my right shoulder. Maybe melodious
Echoes will wing into your white spaces
Where otherworlds form, where sounds
Gather to shape you as creator

Ode to the Holy Spirit

As devotee of the divine, I desire to have the
Baptist's eyes, belief a benevolent sky. The
Christ rose from the river of obedience. As
Dove of the sacred you rested on his crown,
Emblem of peace, caretaker of the venerable
Fire. To your poet you reveal the sempiternal,
God's deepest sighs, wind that assures the
Hearing cry. Reduced to the least, I implore
In depths, pliant as water, uttering the name
"Jesus" as salve. I'm the man born blind,
Keeping to myself. I'm the roadside beggar,
Lazarus who died, the centurion's servant, the
Man with leprosy. I'm the cripple on Sabbath Day,
Nicodemus who at last is born of the spirit.
Of sentiency I'm the human partaker. To the
Paraclete, prayer: let comfort be a starry night,
Quietness a dawn drizzle. I'm more broken,
Rippled with pains, because I'm everyone, all
Silences becoming my self-negating voice.
Teach that I may endure. Unfold that I may
Understand. Grace as the new bloom, light the
Verity to my heart's pond, a pebble like
Wisdom. Rest is a rainforest fountain, an
Exultation beautiful as the flight of swans. I
Yearn for your gifts to vision, seeing your
Zeniths with humilities of the anointed

To the Miracle Plant

Your leaves stem my blood's
Sweet rise, melt fats,
Return clarity to my eyes.
Gynura Procumbens, Longevity
Spinach, Green Harmony –

Your names. Your cut branches
Growing roots in water in days.
Mind-restorative: waking with
Roosters, replanting, slow
Chewing.

Verdure, the garden's light-
Nervured corners, my cantabile
Forest to hear the heart's
Hermit thrushes, or ponder:
If I could regrow

Parts of me, I could give
Myself like petiole – to papa's
Younger sister, a new liver,
To mom's elder sister
New kidneys

On the Balcony

Beethoven knew my life
Would take this turn and slow,
Seeing me leaning for hours
Watching window panes turn
White from yellow, then gray,
Listening again and again
To how he emptied the music
Of its vast and endless longings.
He waited for night's sacramental
Wafer to appear in the window,
Its full light on the piano.
He had become deaf, yet how
Clearly he heard it hold, the way
It asked him to be on the balcony
As it drifted in the cold.
That was when his sonata
Slowed, diminished notes
Bridging centuries, finding me
Through the wish wormhole.

Stars are now lonelier together,
The wind spreading a promise of net
It won't keep. Silence doesn't mean
Cicadas have stopped singing,
City lights keeping vigil growing
Fewer, fewer with sonata ending.
Gravity is the Earth's tongue.
I am the elevated host,
Consecrated for the pavement's
Yearn for communion.

To the Red Fire Monkey

Ama*, papa's mom who loved me more than anyone,
Blamed the year I was born – 1968 – her ethnic
Chinese biases answering why unruliness ruled our home.
Disciplining me was possible when she's not around,
Every now and then belt coiled round papa's hand. Her
Firstborn, papa's elder brother, tied my wrist to the
Grillwork after I instigated my younger cousin to
Hose the floor with our piss. Uncle must have known
It was a mistake when Ama arrived home. What he did
Jerked the dragon in grandma's heart and she fumed,
Knifing her eldest son's authority with scary scolds. "Your
love for that 'monkey' is spoiling him!" I remember
My uncle's words as he argued. My grades began to
Nosedive, report cards decorated with red numbers
Of failing marks, papa and mom like patrons of the
Principal's office. Nicknamed "Monkey" I skipped
Quizzes, classes. Forward ten years or so and I was a
Red as shiver junkie smoking for decades, my life like
Siesta hours of childhood that seldom knew silence.
This year, 2016, how many children, born of red and fire,
Unleashing monkey business as homage to you? How
Vicious can playfulness be? Red and Fire seem
Worse enough. Add Monkey to the mix and all
Expectations fly out the window like banana peels,
Your year guaranteed with the funniest brow raisers,
Zaniest behaviors as cure-all for conformists

Ama is how I addressed my grandmother

Archivist

"Afterlife" needs redefinition when this technology
Becomes public. We're pioneers of preserving
Consciousness. First among equals, Jobs, his mind
Downloaded and stored before his brain and body
Expired, the virtual Steve now omnipresent: we've seen
Forms of otherworlds he sees – as presentations of
Gripping colorations, or it's his imagination. Kaleidoscopic
Holograms suggest lilts and lurements of language:
(I thought I saw Einstein and his smazed smile.) My
Job ensures the Visionary Minds database workable,
Keeping snapshots of next realms like abstractions,
Loading the right consciousness for consultations. The
Mind of Steve Jobs has been uploaded dozens of times,
Norms of his thinking for epigenetic algorithms. I
Offset my aloneness manning digital shelves, writing
Poetry as caffeine for boredom. I wonder if my poems are
Quixotic enough to earn me a place next to Heaney and
Rich, their new poems from the beyond haunting my
Sleepiness. Diabetes overrunning my body, taking its
Toll on physicality. Could my work or poems secure the
Understanding that my senses be saved, here?
Vanity. My role doesn't require exotic skills.
When I leave this body I won't want to be summoned by
Expectations. I've neither answers nor achievements, only
Years of perseverance. They want prophecy from poets,
Zones of mind whose accuracies proceed from words

Teacher

Astuteness of flowers is my law of attraction, for
Bee is the mind in belief's absence, without the
Causalities of a caterpillar. Stems look sturdy,
Drawing to its unperturbed illusion, roots and the
Eternal meeting halfway. I've nothing more to
Finish, nothing new to say. I suggest, but won't
Go past the butterfly, and I never point the way
Home, for that is the task of mountains, what is
Intuited by rivers, still trustworthy stars. I'm still a
Jongleur at heart, traveling in my mind, and
Knowledge used to shine. I was faithful to the
Luminous, seeing no distinctions between the
Marvelous and pebbles, and emeralds were
Numinous. And then the blinding levity of the
Ordinary, the way leaves droop to the sunset,
Perhaps the summit of a lifetime's discoveries,
Quests that at last rest on simplicities, some
Returning, turtledove coos of remembering. If
Solitude were the vastest space of knowing,
Tabula rasa is among the aims, the way true
Understanding slides into a dew of silence.
Vision is verity's soil, and above the toil is
Wonder – warmth and clouds – passing to
Exit the day, fading greens, shimmering whites.
Years nurture the sacred outdoor dwelling, and
Zen is stillness with sounds of water flowing

POETICS

if you cut a stone
into the blue sky's pendant
it must house a star

Homer

For Derek Walcott,
23 January 1930 – 17 March 2017

You have to be half awake
Precarious as vernaculars
Of light

You have to bring the startle
To the shadow
And shelter
The word that sits
On your tongue

For each wish
You are allowed
One pebble

You have to keep slow

Before a stillness
Before a step
And a goldening tree

You have to follow
The river
Past its shoulder

And see

Healer

Apprenticeship to nature a lifetime's work, the
Body like design's tree, yearn to learn like
Caterpillar. Notice symbiosis like trees: don't
Disharmonize flesh-and-blood ecosystems, nor
Exclude the bone's impulse for symmetry. See how
Foliation seeks the sun as if to leaves light
Grants growing harmonies the skyward dance.
Higher in the fractal order, clouds move
In time with cooing from branches. Be
Joyful in watching, and the cosmos will echo itself:
Keep the body within what it needs to repair itself.
Likelihood is what it needs. The grazing cow knows this.
Migratory birds search it. Herbs and spices give it.
Night offers prayer's vocabularies, stars colored as
Olive oil. Every student of healing gains from
Partnership like cultivation to soil. Be
Quiet like the enriching earth. Water your
Roots with love. Do the same with the body.
Source your strength higher. Believe in
Touch as mother to energy. Moringa leaves
Use the hand's work, moringa leaves like hands.
Visualize transformations, the body's return to
Wholeness. Be the ocean for oneness, and
Expect with a grateful heart. Be still and close
Your eyes. Intercede like broth, with your
Zeal in invoking the words for recovery

RIDDLE

after Phantom Limb, digital artwork
by ***Janna Añonuevo Langholz***

The tree shows its neon apple-green branch
for fifteen minutes only, in the interlude
between gloaming and nightfall, when black
leaves court the sky to deepen its blue.

You have to arrive on time, choose the right
spot for viewing. But to know the answer
to the question you must have felt starlight
at least twice in your veins. You must have

dug deeper than roots where electricity
waits for the call home. Beethoven knew
moonlight's solitude. So should you.
You must decipher the owl's elegy

for what you thought you left behind
for your heart to be lighter. You mustn't
leave after you've seen, but wait for the
bonfire to expel its last breath as whisper.

KITE

I
wondered
how the place
would look like from
above. I created an out of
body bird from bamboo and
wallpaper, attached it to
a string. Guiding it
with a blanked
mind,
I let
the
wind
lift
it
higher
then
closed
my
eyes

The Soloist

The wailing voice he freed from his Stradivarius
Slicing their composure like stem, the bow
Seesawing on strings fiddling roots of longing.
The way he snapped and scattered sonata's twigs,
The rosined sound, like sword of a samurai
Swaying to the mind's winds. Grace of hip
Swivels as eyes in the dark coveted the lover
Behind the trills. They swore the bartender
Appeared in the painting behind him when
He squeezed unripe notes. The nun heard her
Unborn child cry. Asked which part fluttered
The candles' pulped scents, old folks recalled.
Doubting the warbler's marble stare,
The widow's face soured, as if she tasted
Midnight's rind. The actors sat till cockcrow,
Stunned like the goldfish that stopped breathing
For a minute after the slowing arpeggios.
The poet was found hanging upstairs,
By a thread the unfinished poem cursing
God for not making his body a violin.
Remembering the way to the shoal, they
Spent all week resetting their timepieces.
And the orchard keeps cracking, yesterday's
Piths pushing up, zests of an end's parting
Lingering in the air – orphaned by his
Heart beating for someone elsewhere.

ONE

To be closer to his material, flour.
Trial and error taught him to layer,
Taught him to crisp or soften surfaces.

Pages prodding *try* the pita, grissini, Stollen,
Zwieback, *try* new forms, flavored crusts,
Hues of black forest, brown, gold.

Shaping finger rolls like painting
Inscapes, hand movements hypnotic,
Inward rolls rhythmic.

Baguettes lengthen his meditations.
He braids concentration like Challah,
Sprinkling poppy seeds on plaits.

Cottage, Vienna, fruit, farmhouse
Loaves. Each croissant like a face
He loved. Self-portraits of wheat, rye.

Imagining the peel in his powdered hands,
Visualizing larger fire, basil and garlic
Filling the room with changed air

Spreading marmalades of recall
On toast: aroma of the father imago –
Why he became artificer of dough.

This morning, before the painters arrived,
He tried his self-taught measure on *pan de sal*.
One failed to rise to the desired size

Yet no other held longer his
Rumination to his artistic flaws,
No other point angled the interior light.

Ode to Green Tea

Legend: your wind-plucked leaf finding
The golden cup, greening the cooling water,
Fragrant balm to the emperor Shennong.
Your sprouts garland the slopes of China,
Japan, India, Sri Lanka, handpicked

From dawn's dew-decked beds, shoots
Longing for rain song, buds on bamboo
Trays quenching the sun's thirst.
Small cloth or paper bags hold essences,
Steeping my mornings with jasmine scents.

I sip to wellness, inhaling good health's
Shy urgings, worries swept to the edges.
I sip to music, hearing the heart's
Hermit thrushes, arias in trees.
I sip, infusing mind with word silences

From pages: reading and writing poetry like
Cultivating my own *Camellia Sinensis* garden.
It will take years to grow a good crop,
Years of pruning, soil conditioning,
Quiet joy in the harvesting.

Echo

The morning's speaker talks about
moments of loss, but you're here
in this retreat of bamboo and nipa
to remember and compose
grief's letter.

After lunch you linger by the well.
It's easy to see how stillness
repeats the sky, how water
can turn pebble into an eye.
You recall your father show
that hills have voice.
You call out his name, and smile.

The lady calls for afternoon session to start
but odd and even lines are rhyming.
You sit under the dovecote. A stray wind
spreads a jolt of carabao dung, crackles
firewood. The tree sends a greeting
of leaves to the passing stream.
You sense grasses parting, glad your
turn doesn't conjure your fear.

Three more lines for the sonnet
as the bonfire begins, star-attended singing
and sharing. Darkness in the house reminds
of what your father did after drinking:
you'd stagger and stir kitchen smells and sounds
and be gone by the time I like a mouse
wake hungry and reach that part of the house.

Thirteen Ways of Looking

1. rain singing all week
   heart's hermit thrush
   voiceless

2. taste of tea
   white as perched
   serendipity

3. fiction writing –
   indoor branches
   for angelic beings

4. insight:
   elusive
   flowerpecker

5. raindrops
   too many commas
   for a fruitless day

6. smell of coffee...
   memory
   drinking from its feathers

7. chirps in the downpour –
   mind full
   Of parables

8. curtain turning like a page...
   where's the pterodactyl
   in the mirror?

9. window
   with tricks of trees –
   foretelling sparrows

10. hot cocoa...
    metaphors following flocks
    searching their songleader

11. I don't know which to prefer, woods for my winged beings or a poem with moon in the pond. I rummage my drawers for the winter we don't have, well-versed in the monsoon's dialogues with our summer sun glowing like Mandarin orange. To imagine the dry spell, I try iced and milked blends: cantaloupe-papaya, apple-soursop, dragon fruit-mango.

>   Odus the Owl…
>   darkened room
>   for nestled warmth

12. Butterflies on my vision's
    hibiscus: echoes
    of the storm's beauty

13. Maybe the songbird
    was the orange light
    on the field of grass

*Odus the Owl is part of the popular game Candy Crush Saga

Flute for His Newborn

He asked for the bamboo's benevolence –
The plea for forest spirits to hear – sawing
With remorseful care, the form's slender
Whisper sending joy of discovery farther
Than the turtledoves. For days he hallowed;
With the steel rod's fire he hollowed the reed.
Thinking of him, he burned out the holes,
Feeling if pain's tinniest slivers would groan
To his fingers. Carving, praying for
Forgiveness for wounding the dried flesh
With his art's depths. When winds
Stopped blowing, he descended
And traveled for miles to the city
To find the kind of varnish
That deepens the sun's shadows.

If the boy picks it up one day
He'll know it pines for his breathing.
He'll have his own forest rhythms,
Or the miles of wind-raked fields
In his heart every son is born with.

Tao of Indoor Walk

Moving, reverential pacing, in minimalist sounds, under an
Incense-colored ceiling, mist like the wind's inverness. The
Numinous slakes like water's lulling murmur. I'm lesser than
Dewdrops on stones, as I circle barefoot on marble. Here,
Shadows home in rituals of summer. My heart dwells with
Chirps from trees older than my grandparents, melodious.
Attuned, I tie ribbons of my gratefulness to the bonsai
Pruned between prayer and the moon's passage,
Each reclaimed step a hymn to solitude

Nonfiction

If before midnight you catch a sight
    of the golden leaf gliding into the well,
        return by the moon's lent light knowing
all is well, your prayer water stilled. What the wind
picks from the weary bough and tosses
    in your way,
        consume.
Love might keep the candles burning.
        The nightingale might sing.

Lovers in a Fresco

We're glorified in his fame's afterglow.
As his mind's depths and shades of indigo,
We're one, talking of Michelangelo.

Beneath Bartholomew's flayed skin is blue,
The artist's deep yearns fleshed with nude yellow.
Angels glory in his light's afterglow.

The snake coiled round Minos, as prayers flow,
Silence solemn as candles in their glow:
We breathe, dreaming of Michelangelo.

In our congregation blends the rainbow –
Oranges, hues of the virtuoso,
How he colored our delight's afterglow

And the grays, the whites, the body's shadow.
Peter, Paul, John, Lawrence and the widow
Of Joseph, Christ of Michelangelo –

We sing the artist's desires, and we bow.
The rich, the poor, the colored come and go,
Gloried in the faith and its afterglow,
In God's house – dome of Michelangelo.

In My View

Time passes as palomino in summer,
In the rainy season roan, always entire,
Never jade, balky not just at midlife,
Eye-catching musculature between
Crupper and hock, withers and pastern,
Strength difficult to hamshackle.

Decades ago, the *tartanilla* lumbered,
Papa beside me, paying the old man
To steer the two-wheel carriage back
And forth Sanciangko. This riding stilled me,
Not the view, my curiosity on the beast of burden.
Smell of manure remains, memory of
Papa sober, showing his five year old son
The timeless way. In my adolescence
With my own races, I never heard hooves.

Halfway through my fifth decade
I feel my body clocks slowing
And how it speeds in my view. How long
Do I still measure its circles in minutes?
The more days race into my years
The faster it disappears.

Piano

Papa paid for my lessons with the only lady
Who ever slapped my hand with a ruler:
I wasn't supposed to play the piece that fast,
My hands so small I had to catch up, turning
Chords into arpeggios, false impression of speed.
She should have heard how I improvised.
She was so strict I played the *Fur Elise* like my
Fingers were birds flying to her thick glasses.

Perhaps when drunk papa saw me a pianist,
Melody engraver who might halt passersby,
Listeners keeping their hearts in brocaded boxes.
Then my training stopped when he stopped
Leaving the house when his sobriety stopped.
He had to sell it or we would stop schooling,
My brother and I, we would starve. The truck
That took it lumbered like a groggy box, the space
It left in our house I still keep in my heart.

STORM

An
eye
opening, twirling
      sky's Ferris Wheel
            nature's whistling top, cosmic dervish

    choral lightning and thunder, the window and my
view of beauty, and I see, and I see, and I see

The Great Barrier Reef

This morning I read about The Great Barrier Reef
Dying due to climate change, marine life kaleidoscopes
Bleaching, as if white were capitulation's color,
The Earth spotted with sadness no ocean can blue,
Aquamarine greenness a distant memory.

I picture the body's anatomy, branched like full-grown
Corals, young immune system like a reef to algae
And symbiotic sunlight. I imagine decades of neglect,
Greed and abuse, coldness to pleasure's consequences
Altering colors to bruise violets, tumor pinks,

Reds and grays of foreseeable acquiescence.
But the human body is resilient and restorative,
A metaphor showing shoals and lagoons,
The deep sea cave in the ribcage, islets, and
The way it heals itself as model or design.

Pictures of the Floating World

1.

If you
are the breadwinner, you
are jolted by its arrival roofs announce. You
rush out, risking salted fish to fizz to embers,
kettle to hiss and spew coconut milk,
to unburden clotheslines.

Returning, you
see the snoring still sprawled. You
drop your sartorial rage, your
whitened, sun-dried, wash-and-wear discontent,
hosiery of regret and innocence remembered
dull against the dream-burdened floor.

The wall's subfusk: clock
saying schoolboys will arrive anytime like
exhausted runners in a four hundred-meter dash.

2.

If you
are a researcher from the DENR, a semblance
of white noise jolts you. You
look around for everybody. You
save the files properly. You
step out of the office to ease your
neck; light a cigarette to thaw
artificial cold swathing your
body like ague.

Outside, it has reached crescendo
connoting, based on experience, a near ending.
A thought interlude of something you,
trusting the morning, decided not to bring.

Looking at the plaza from the town hall, you imagine underground clogs and blockages.

3.

If you are an eight-year old, you
start to shiver, suck thumb as the other hand

keeps the garterless from falling. You
are stuck in gray matter flowing, risen
like kundalini to hide your
shins but not from imagined moccasins. You
have been wondering with what
to replace the shoelace you
lost – to ease the other hand.

Your partners in play wade among flotsam,
deaf to angry voices competing with
drowning trikes from Capiz windows.

Like entering satori, you smile, your
eyes trailing a yellow Volkswagen beetle
pushed among pushcarts of hot peanuts and tempura,
the owner smiling a wry thanksgiving
for bystanders' muscle.

4.

If you
are a college student, disembarking the jeepney
at the terminal with great relief, you
take off your
polo, use it to wipe your
hair and body, forgetting you
put in its pocket the lotto tickets you
have to give to your
father at dinner.

5.

If the three of
you are huddled hungry in a nipa hut,
you take turns protecting with
your hands or with one of the T-shirts –
the candleflame and the secret samadhi of plates.

6.

If you
are side dish of gossip, perhaps this cliché
is neither fiction nor poetry:
That you lost your job. A year later, your
Freyja left, with your
twin Fauntleroys. It was only *a matter of time,*

neighbors said, before whatever – would drive you...

here.
You smile in the candle's noetic light. You
clear the table: plastic plates, T-shirt, shorts
and underwear like islets. You
should have hours ago started working with
the plastic pitcher or dustpan.

But you
believe the arrived has the heart to also leave.
A longneck bottle of cheap rum, heavy on your
head like pieces of *carenderia* paper with your
signature kept among money in the till, makes you
believe in the Savior's soliloquy: The spirit
is willing. Monotony seems to prolong, nay
encourage, what housewives call
self-hypnosis, while you
lie spread-eagle under a tearful ceiling. You
play oblivious to the risen with mind and soul
to wash whatever away or like eudaemon, to embrace.

7.

If you are sleepless in your bower, you
open your
favorite book and listen to the poet
in a banquet of candlelight.

A cold finger traces your
spine luring centipedes from under your
skin: It isn't the poet you
recognize.

8.

If your
husband and only child were found
three days after that infamous shipwreck
two years ago, this is your
third night in a friend's cottage.
She was shocked to see you
a skeletal, monosyllabic paraphrase of the
incandescent plum glowing pink last year at your
kid sister's wedding

To bring yourself from bed to bamboo bench
in the veranda requires will and strength
And the world is
the sound of something steady
the wind's vibraharp the leaves' ashram bells
the sound of nothing behind nothing – you

are jolted by the post glowering

You
see the garden's waggery of verdigris

9.

"*Poor savage, doubting that a river flows*‖"
                        —James Merrill

If you
are still listening, can you hear the Big Dipper's mandala?

Can you hear the mimosa
imitating the earth's heart chakra?

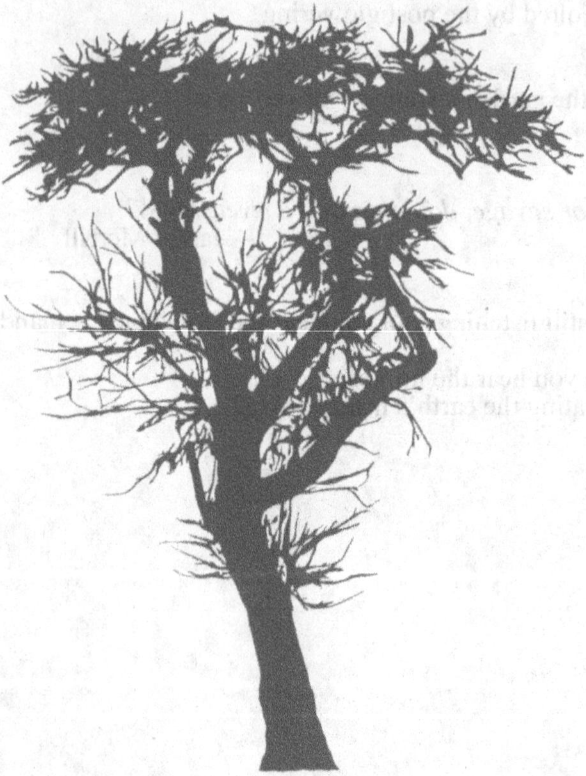

Ode to the Moon

Apogee, as when you long for the galaxies,
Barely reflecting for my wonder the way your
Crescent smile augurs the fisherman's skiff or
Diana with bow and arrows. In the canvass you
Evince my wishes. I return and rise from
Forks of dreaming to be here in artificial
Gibbous light. Three sweepers haunt the street,
Harvesting leaves trees shed this summer,
In wee hours baring sidewalks and pavements,
Janitorial diligence the only stirrings. I'll
Keep them in mind as Cynthia, Phoebe, Selene,
Later add them to the picture where you
Might be sensed beyond the boundaries:
Not seen, your fullness, but light unmistakable.
Over brushstrokes shimmer hints of your
Presence, your silvering shades stilling
Questions. This immaterial hour invites the ear,
Renews the strolling wind's immanence over
Silences. They move, chores separate but
Together following rhythms of broomsticks.
Until I alter my images with solitude, I'll
Venture on. You'll be round someplace,
Waxing or in perigee. I imagine how
Xanthic their parts in your company,
Yellowish their nightcaps in life's stopovers:
Zinfandel or whiskey, beer or brandy

38

Jonel Abellanosa resides in Cebu City, The Philippines. His poetry has appeared in numerous journals and anthologies, and been nominated for the *Pushcart Prize, Dwarf Stars and Best of the Net Awards*. *Songs from My Mind's Tree* is his fourth chapbook. His full-length poetry collection, *Multiverse* was published by Clare Songbirds Publishing House, New York in 2018

www.ingramcontent.com/pod-product-compliance
Lightning Source LLC
Chambersburg PA
CBHW012007120526
44592CB00040B/2657